The State Of Alabama

Community Foundations

Local, Regional Scholarships, Grants

Scholarship Search Workbook

this book belongs to

_____

Graduate.
Debt-Free.

The goal of this publication is to help you graduate without a huge debt. It's that simple.

Our goal is to expose you to the many local and regional opportunities to apply for and win grants and scholarships - in your local community.

<u>National</u> scholarships get attention because of the large amount of scholarship money involved. Only a few have a chance. Competition is fierce.

We introduce local and regional opportunities to get smaller scholarships. Some are never claimed.

The money is out there. Do the groundwork now. Graduate debt-free. It will transform your life!

KENNETH EDLIN
Research Analyst
Debt-Free College Graduate

© Copyright. All Rights Reserved

National Scholarships vs Community Foundation Scholarships

National Scholarships

- open to all students nationwide

- offered by Government agencies, Corporations and Organizations

- extremely competitive

- strict adherence to rules and deadlines

- low acceptance rates

- focus on prestige

Community Foundations

- limited to students in specific geographical local areas

- offered by regional, local business and entities

- less competitive

- flexible timelines

- some scholarships never applied for

- focus on helping local students

The Sad Truth About Student Loans

The easy way to get through college <u>often</u> becomes a debt that never goes away. It's what will keep your family in debt well into middle age. Government agencies and financial institutions will have their hand out on all your future earnings because of the compounding student loan debt you allowed them to talk you into at the college financial office. Bankruptcy will not eliminate it. Do the work now.

What Are Community Foundations

What Community Foundations Do

Community foundations are local organizations that help people in a community by managing money and resources for charitable purposes.

One of the main things they do is provide scholarships to help students pay for college or specialized education.

How Community Foundations Help with Scholarships

Manage Scholarship Funds:
- Community foundations take care of money that people or organizations give to help students.//
- This money is set aside specifically for scholarships.

Give Money for School:
- Scholarships from community foundations are like gifts of money that students don't have to pay back.
- They can use this money to cover costs like tuition, books, and fees.

Offer Different Scholarships:
- Many community foundations have several scholarships available, so students can apply for different ones all at once.
- Some scholarships might be for specific types of students, like those going into certain careers or those from particular areas.

What Community Foundations Do
2

Look at More Than Just Grades:
- When deciding who gets scholarships, community foundations often consider more than just grades.

- They want to help students from all backgrounds, so they look at things like community service, personal challenges, and other achievements.

Provide Help and Information:
- Community foundations often have resources to help students understand how to apply for scholarships.

- They might have guides, FAQs, or people you can talk to if you have questions.

Focus on Local Students:
- Many community foundations focus on helping students from their own area, making sure that the scholarships support <u>local</u> kids.

- In short, Community Foundations are important for students because they offer scholarships that help pay for education, making it easier for teens to go to college without worrying about huge debts.

The spotlight is on you to <u>find</u> <u>and</u> <u>apply</u> for FREE scholarship money.

Find Now or Pay More Later

What you need to know:

- Scholarships are FREE money.
- Doing some work now will make a huge difference in your future.
- Many graduates in their 40's and 50's are still paying off their student loans.

- Later in life, your paycheck will not be yours to raise your family; your paycheck will belong to your bank or government.
- Scholarships are out there.
- Some Scholarships remain unclaimed because no one applies for the money.
- It's just too easy to sign up for loans.
- Banks and Government agencies will loan you the money. They get wealthy from the compound interest they charge.
- Your goal is to avoid student debt.

Be Wise. Stay alert!

This book does not address access to Federal money that may be available to you through the FAFSA process.

Grants and other scholarships will be available through your school or college counselors.

This publication seeks to deliver scholarship opportunities available on a local or regional level to you.

Your commitment must be to avoid debt.

It has become the "normal" practice to take out student loans. Schools, banks, and the government make money from students borrowing tuition and living costs.

All student debt must be repaid, and the interest is the dreaded "compound" interest, which means the interest accumulates and becomes a goldmine for the banks.

Even if you go into bankruptcy later, student loans are not wiped out. You are the fish on the hook. Do the work now. Stay out of debt.

First! <u>Ask</u> for Potential <u>Local</u> Scholarship Leads

1

- [ ] High School Guidance Counselor. Ask for lists of <u>Local</u> <u>Grants</u> and <u>Scholarships.</u>

- [ ] Go to <u>ALL</u> High School Guidance offices in your School District. Many Counselors will have lists of scholarships that are "different."

- [ ] Ask about "old" or "expired" scholarships that can possibly be renewed.

- [ ] Accept <u>small</u> amounts. $500 scholarships add up. There is less competition for smaller amounts.

- [ ] Ask "two" questions - 1. How many applied last year? 2. How many awards for this year?

- [ ] Why? Jump quickly on the scholarships that only a "few" applied for last year! Less competition.

- [ ] <u>Cold</u> call numerous business owners in your town. Some may respond positively for you.

- [ ] Join Clubs and Organizations that offer potential scholarships. Creates a potential advantage.

- [ ] Locate Civic Groups in your town or city. Ask what they may consider offering to you.

- [ ] Big businesses or successful business owners in town or large groups like Coca-Cola, Tylenol, and Microsoft have in-house Charitable Foundations."

First! Look for Potential <u>Local</u> Scholarship Leads

2

- [ ] If your parents or grandparents <u>are or were</u> in Military Service.

- [ ] Find out if they offer scholarships where your parents or family work.

- [ ] Working part-time? Wegmans gave 1,900 employee scholarships in 2022. Ask. Find out.

- [ ] Accept small amounts. $500 scholarships add up. There is less competition for smaller amounts.

- [ ] Are your parents associated with a Union? Ask if they offer scholarships.

- [ ] Look at each High School's website for possible scholarship listings.

- [ ] Does your parent's employer offer scholarships to their employee's children?

- [ ] Performing Art Centers may offer scholarships for future musicians.

- [ ] Ask at your place of worship. Religious Groups, Churches, Synagogues, Mosques.

- [ ] <u>Community Foundations.</u> We have a complete section on these State resources for <u>local</u> and <u>regional</u> scholarships that are available.

First! Look for Potential <u>Local</u> Scholarship Leads
3

- [ ] Does your local School District have a Community Foundation list of local Scholarships? Ask.

- [ ] Find out if local chapters of large organizations have local scholarships. Such as the Elks Clubs.

- [ ] Check local City, County, and State Government offices for scholarship listings.

- [ ] Check your local Department of Education's website for local listings for your town, or city.

- [ ] Ask local Utility companies what they have available for <u>future</u> employment opportunities.

- [ ] Ask doctors groups of all kinds if you have a desire to enter that occupation in the future.

- [ ] Many lawyers offer potential employees <u>summer internships</u> or opportunities.

- [ ] Some Library systems that want potential employees may be able to find scholarship funds.

- [ ] Some local Banks, Credit Unions, and financial institutions may have scholarships available.

- [ ] Car Dealerships may be willing to sponsor a scholarship if they are approached. They may see something you are studying to pique their interest.

First! Look for Potential <u>Local</u> Scholarship Leads

4

- [ ] Media. Radio and television stations are often looking for potentially talented employees.

- [ ] Explore websites of <u>local</u> Colleges and Universities for scholarship information or opportunities.

- [ ] Contact the financial office of <u>local</u> universities and colleges and ask for scholarship lists.

- [ ] Equestrian Organizations and Amateur Sports Groups may have funds for local students.

- [ ] Ask Boy Scouts and Girl Scouts leadership if they have programs or scholarship money available.

- [ ] College Alumni Groups may have information or a willingness to make contacts for you if you ask.

- [ ] Make contact with local hospitals if you are pursuing a career in medicine.

- [ ] Contact the <u>local</u> Chamber of Commerce for lists of scholarships or business contacts available.

- [ ] Some local <u>Bulletin Boards</u> can be a goldmine. Put your contact information where it may be found.

- [ ] American Legion, American Red Cross, 4-H Clubs, the Lions Club, Junior Leagues International, and Athletic Booster Clubs are all worth pursuing...

Work Sheets

- [ ] _____
- [ ] _____
- [ ] _____
- [ ] _____
- [ ] _____
- [ ] _____
- [ ] _____

Get Organized.

Scholarship Search Individual Work Sheet

Name of Potential Scholarship Date:

_____   _____

Source

_____

Notes

Required Action

- [ ] _____
- [ ] _____
- [ ] _____
- [ ] _____
- [ ] _____
- [ ] _____
- [ ] _____

Results

_____
_____
_____
_____
_____
_____

Scholarship Search Individual Work Sheet

Name of Potential Scholarship

Date:

Source

Notes

Required Action

- [ ] _____
- [ ] _____
- [ ] _____
- [ ] _____
- [ ] _____
- [ ] _____
- [ ] _____

Results

_____
_____
_____
_____
_____
_____
_____

Scholarship Search Individual Work Sheet

Name of Potential Scholarship Date:
_____ _____

Source
_____

Notes

Required Action

☐ _____
☐ _____
☐ _____
☐ _____
☐ _____
☐ _____
☐ _____

Results

_____
_____
_____
_____
_____
_____
_____

Scholarship Search Individual Work Sheet

Name of Potential Scholarship
_____

Date:
_____

Source
_____

Notes

Required Action

- [ ] _____
- [ ] _____
- [ ] _____
- [ ] _____
- [ ] _____
- [ ] _____
- [ ] _____

Results

_____
_____
_____
_____
_____
_____
_____

Scholarship Search Individual Work Sheet

Name of Potential Scholarship   Date:
_____   _____

Source
_____

Notes

Required Action

☐ _____
☐ _____
☐ _____
☐ _____
☐ _____
☐ _____
☐ _____

Results

_____
_____
_____
_____
_____
_____

20

Scholarship Search Individual Work Sheet

Name of Potential Scholarship Date:

Source

Notes

Required Action

- [ ]
- [ ]
- [ ]
- [ ]
- [ ]
- [ ]
- [ ]

Results

U.S. States Community Foundations Local Scholarships, Grants

<u>Alabama</u>	North Carolina
Alaska	North Dakota
Arizona	New England
Arkansas	New Hampshire
California	New Jersey
Colorado	New Mexico
Connecticut	Nevada
Washington D.C.	New York
Delaware	Ohio
Florida	Oklahoma
Georgia	Oregon
Hawaii	Pennsylvania
Iowa	Puerto Rico
Idaho	Rhode Island
Illinois	South Carolina
Kansas	South Dakota
Kentucky	Tennessee
Louisiana	Texas
Massachusetts	Utah
Maryland	Virginia
Maine	Virgin Islands
Michigan	Vermont
Minnesota	Washington
Missouri	Wisconsin
Mississippi	West Virginia
Montana	Wyoming

Community Foundation

<u>Alabama</u>

1

Community Foundation of South Alabama

Website: communityfoundationsa.org
(251) 438-5591
Email: info@communityfoundationsa.org

Notes

- [ ] _____
- [ ] _____
- [ ] _____
- [ ] _____
- [ ] _____
- [ ] _____
- [ ] _____

Results

Community Foundation

Alabama
2

<u>Community Foundation of Greater Birmingham [CFGB]</u>

Website: cfbham.org
(205) 327-3800
Email: info@cfbham.org
2100 First Avenue North, Birmingham, AL 35203

Information Notes

- [ ] _____
- [ ] _____
- [ ] _____
- [ ] _____
- [ ] _____
- [ ] _____
- [ ] _____

Results

_____
_____
_____
_____
_____

Community Foundation

<u>Alabama</u>
3

<u>Community Foundation of Northeast Alabama [CFNEA]</u>

Website: yourcommunityfirst.org
(256) 231-5160
Email: info@cfnea.org
1130 Quintard Avenue, Suite 100, Anniston, AL 36201

Information Notes

- [ ] _____
- [ ] _____
- [ ] _____
- [ ] _____
- [ ] _____
- [ ] _____
- [ ] _____

Results

Community Foundation
Alabama
4

Community Foundation of West Alabama [CFWA]

Website: thecfwa.org
(205) 366-0698
Email: info@thecfwa.org
2720 6th Street, Suite 100, Tuscaloosa, AL 35401

Information Notes

- [ ] _____
- [ ] _____
- [ ] _____
- [ ] _____
- [ ] _____
- [ ] _____
- [ ] _____

Results

_____
_____
_____
_____
_____

Community Foundation

Alabama
5

Central Alabama Community Foundation[CACF]

Website: cacfinfo.org
(334) 264-6223
Email: info@cacfinfo.org
114 Church Street, Montgomery, AL 36104

Information Notes

☐ _____
☐ _____
☐ _____
☐ _____
☐ _____
☐ _____
☐ _____

Results

_____
_____
_____
_____
_____

Community Foundation

Alabama
6

Black Belt Community Foundation[BBCF]

Website: blackbeltfound.org
(334) 874-1126
Email: info@blackbeltfound.org
609 Lauderdale Street, Selma, AL 36701

Information Notes

☐ _____
☐ _____
☐ _____
☐ _____
☐ _____
☐ _____
☐ _____

Results

Community Foundation

Alabama
7

Walker Area Community Foundation

Website: wacf.org
(205) 302-0001
Email: info@wacf.org
124 N. Walston Bridge Rd, Jasper, AL 35504

Information Notes

- [ ] _____
- [ ] _____
- [ ] _____
- [ ] _____
- [ ] _____
- [ ] _____
- [ ] _____

Results

Community Foundation

<u>Alabama</u>
8

<u>Community Foundation of Greater Huntsville</u>

Website: communityfoundationhsv.org
(256) 564-7430
Email: info@communityfoundationhsv.org
303 N. Williams Avenue, Suite 1031, Huntsville, AL 35801

Information Notes

- [ ] _____
- [ ] _____
- [ ] _____
- [ ] _____
- [ ] _____
- [ ] _____
- [ ] _____

Results

_____
_____
_____
_____

30

Community Foundation

Alabama
9

Community Foundation of East Alabama [CFEA]

Website: cfeastalabama.org
(334) 705-5138
Email: info@cfeastalabama.org
2353 Bent Creek Rd, Suite 100, Auburn, AL 36830

Information Notes

- [ ] _____
- [ ] _____
- [ ] _____
- [ ] _____
- [ ] _____
- [ ] _____
- [ ] _____

Results

Community Foundation

Alabama
10

Limestone Area Community Foundation

Website: athenslimestonefoundation.com
(256) 232-1234
Email: info@athenslimestonefoundation.com
P.O. Box 1644, Athens, AL 35612

Information Notes

- [ ] _____
- [ ] _____
- [ ] _____
- [ ] _____
- [ ] _____
- [ ] _____
- [ ] _____

Results

_____
_____
_____
_____
_____

Community Foundation
<u>Alabama</u>
11

<u>The Community Foundation of Greater Decatur</u>

Website: cfdecatur.org
(256) 353-5312
Email: info@cfdecatur.org
352 Moulton Street, Suite D, Decatur, AL 35601

Information Notes

☐ _____
☐ _____
☐ _____
☐ _____
☐ _____
☐ _____
☐ _____

Results

Community Foundation

Alabama

12

Community Foundation of Calhoun County

Website: cfcalhoun.org
(256) 238-8363
Email: info@cfcalhoun.org
1330 Quintard Avenue, Anniston, AL 36201

Information Notes

☐ _____
☐ _____
☐ _____
☐ _____
☐ _____
☐ _____
☐ _____

Results

_____
_____
_____
_____
_____

Community Foundation

Alabama
13

Shoals Area Community Foundation

Website: shoalsfoundation.org
(256) 764-5869
Email: info@shoalsfoundation.org
128 South Court Street, Florence, AL 35630

Information Notes

- [ ] _____
- [ ] _____
- [ ] _____
- [ ] _____
- [ ] _____
- [ ] _____
- [ ] _____

Results

Community Foundation

Alabama

14

Community Foundation of Etowah County

Website: cfetowah.org
(256) 543-7403
Email: info@cfetowah.org
1130 Quintard Avenue, Suite 100, Anniston, AL 36201

Information Notes

- [ ] _____
- [ ] _____
- [ ] _____
- [ ] _____
- [ ] _____
- [ ] _____
- [ ] _____

Results

Community Foundation

Alabama
15

Autauga Area Community Foundation

Website: autaugacommunityfoundation.org
(334) 358-0297
Email: info@autaugacommunityfoundation.org
135 North Court Street, Prattville, AL 36067

Information Notes

☐ _____
☐ _____
☐ _____
☐ _____
☐ _____
☐ _____
☐ _____

Results

_____
_____
_____
_____
_____

Community Foundation

Alabama
16

Elmore County Community Foundation

Website: elmorecountycommunityfoundation.org
(334) 567-4076
Email: info@elmorecountycommunityfoundation.org
131 Main Street, Wetumpka, AL 36092

Information Notes

- [ ] _____
- [ ] _____
- [ ] _____
- [ ] _____
- [ ] _____
- [ ] _____
- [ ] _____

Results

_____
_____
_____
_____

Community Foundation

Alabama
17

Southeast Alabama Community Foundation

Website: southeastalabamacommunityfoundation.org
(334) 792-5138
Email: info@southeastalabamacommunityfoundation.org
188 North Foster Street, Dothan, AL 36303

Information Notes

- [ ] _____
- [ ] _____
- [ ] _____
- [ ] _____
- [ ] _____
- [ ] _____
- [ ] _____

Results

Community Foundation

Alabama
18

Fayette Community Foundation

Website: fayettecommunityfoundation.org
(205) 932-6001
Email: info@fayettecommunityfoundation.org
103 Temple Avenue North, Fayette, AL 35555

Information Notes

- [ ] _____
- [ ] _____
- [ ] _____
- [ ] _____
- [ ] _____
- [ ] _____
- [ ] _____

Results

Community Foundation

<u>Alabama</u>
19

<u>Cleon Jones Last Out Community Foundation</u>

Website: lastoutcommunityfoundation.org
(251) 456-0000
Email: info@lastoutcommunityfoundation.org
123 Main Street, Prichard, AL 36610

Information Notes

- [ ] _____
- [ ] _____
- [ ] _____
- [ ] _____
- [ ] _____
- [ ] _____
- [ ] _____

Results

_____
_____
_____
_____
_____

Community Foundation

Alabama
20

Impact 100 Baldwin County

Website: impact100baldwincounty.org
(251) 990-0000
Email: info@impact100baldwincounty.org
200 South Section Street, Fairhope, AL 36532

Information Notes

- [ ] _____
- [ ] _____
- [ ] _____
- [ ] _____
- [ ] _____
- [ ] _____
- [ ] _____

Results

Community Foundation

<u>Alabama</u>
21

<u>Guin Area Charitable Foundation</u>

Website: not available
(205) 468-0000
Email: info@guincharitablefoundation.org
P.O. Box 278, Guin, AL 35563

Information Notes

Results

Community Foundation

Alabama
22

Capital Heights Civic Association

Website: not available
(334) 000-0000
Email: info@capitalheightscivic.org
123 Capital Heights, Montgomery, AL 36107

Information Notes

☐ _____
☐ _____
☐ _____
☐ _____
☐ _____
☐ _____
☐ _____

Results

_____
_____
_____
_____
_____

Community Foundation

Alabama
23

Lizzie K Welch United Appeal Fund

Website: not available
(334) 727-0000
Email: info@welchappealfund.org
1200 Old Montgomery Highway, Tuskegee, AL 36083

Information Notes

- [ ] _____
- [ ] _____
- [ ] _____
- [ ] _____
- [ ] _____
- [ ] _____
- [ ] _____

Results

Community Foundation

Alabama
24

Double Vision Foundation

Website: not available
(334) 285-0000
Email: info@doublevisionfoundation.org
1500 Highway 14 East, Millbrook, AL 36054

Information Notes

- [ ] _____
- [ ] _____
- [ ] _____
- [ ] _____
- [ ] _____
- [ ] _____
- [ ] _____

Results

_____
_____
_____
_____
_____

Community Foundation

Alabama
25

Alabama Business Charitable Trust Fund

Website: not available
(205) 257-0000
Email: info@abctfund.org
600 North 18th Street, Birmingham, AL 35203

Information Notes

- [ ] _____
- [ ] _____
- [ ] _____
- [ ] _____
- [ ] _____
- [ ] _____
- [ ] _____

Results

_____
_____
_____
_____
_____

Community Foundation

Alabama
26

Etowah Community Foundation

Website: not available
(256) 543-0000
Email: info@etowahcommunityfoundation.org
501 Broad Street, Gadsden, AL 35901

Information Notes

- ☐ _____
- ☐ _____
- ☐ _____
- ☐ _____
- ☐ _____
- ☐ _____
- ☐ _____

Results

_____
_____
_____
_____
_____

Community Foundation

Alabama
27

Hale County Community Foundation

Website: not available
(334) 624-0000
Email: info@halecountyfoundation.org
1001 Main Street, Greensboro, AL 36744

Information Notes

Results

Community Foundation

Alabama
28

Hartselle Area Community Foundation

Website: not available
(256) 773-0000
Email: info@hartsellefoundation.org
100 Sparkman Street, Hartselle, AL 35640

Information Notes

- [ ] _____
- [ ] _____
- [ ] _____
- [ ] _____
- [ ] _____
- [ ] _____
- [ ] _____

Results

_____
_____
_____
_____
_____

50

Community Foundation

Alabama
29

Jackson County Community Foundation

Website: not available
(256) 574-0000
Email: info@jacksoncountyfoundation.org
123 South Broad Street, Scottsboro, AL 35768

Information Notes

- [ ] _____
- [ ] _____
- [ ] _____
- [ ] _____
- [ ] _____
- [ ] _____
- [ ] _____

Results

Community Foundation

Alabama
30

Jefferson County Community Foundation

Website: not available
(205) 325-0000
Email: info@jeffersoncountyfoundation.org
2100 1st Avenue North, Birmingham, AL 35203

Information Notes

- [ ] _____
- [ ] _____
- [ ] _____
- [ ] _____
- [ ] _____
- [ ] _____
- [ ] _____

Results

_____
_____
_____
_____
_____

Community Foundation

Alabama
31

Lauderdale County Community Foundation

Website: not available
(256) 760-0000
Email: info@lauderdalefoundation.org
120 North Wood Avenue, Florence, AL 35630

Information Notes

- [ ] _____
- [ ] _____
- [ ] _____
- [ ] _____
- [ ] _____
- [ ] _____
- [ ] _____

Results

Community Foundation

Alabama
32

Lawrence County Community Foundation

Website: not available
(256) 974-0000
Email: info@lawrencecountyfoundation.org
14451 Market Street, Moulton, AL 35650

Information Notes

☐ _____
☐ _____
☐ _____
☐ _____
☐ _____
☐ _____
☐ _____

Results

_____
_____
_____
_____
_____

Community Foundation

Alabama
33

<u>Lee County Community Foundation</u>

Website: not available
(334) 821-0000
Email: info@leecountyfoundation.org
135 North College Street, Auburn, AL 36830

Information Notes

☐ _____
☐ _____
☐ _____
☐ _____
☐ _____
☐ _____
☐ _____

Results

_____
_____
_____
_____

Community Foundation

Alabama
34

Madison County Community Foundation

Website: not available
(356) 532-0000
Email: info@madisoncountyfoundation.org
123 Church Street, Huntsville, AL 35801

Information Notes

- [ ] _____
- [ ] _____
- [ ] _____
- [ ] _____
- [ ] _____
- [ ] _____
- [ ] _____

Results

_____
_____
_____
_____
_____

Community Foundation

Alabama
35

<u>Marengo County Community Foundation</u>

Website: not available
(334) 295-0000
Email: info@marengofoundation.org
100 East Washington Street, Demopolis, AL 36732

Information Notes

- [ ] _____
- [ ] _____
- [ ] _____
- [ ] _____
- [ ] _____
- [ ] _____
- [ ] _____

Results

Community Foundation

Alabama

36

Marshall County Community Foundation

Website: not available
(256) 382-0000
Email: info@marshallcountyfoundation.org
424 Blount Avenue, Guntersville, AL 35976

Information Notes

☐ _____
☐ _____
☐ _____
☐ _____
☐ _____
☐ _____
☐ _____

Results

_____
_____
_____
_____

Community Foundation

Alabama
37

Mobile County Community Foundation

Website: not available
(251) 208-0000
Email: info@mobilecountyfoundation.org
205 Government Street, Mobile, AL 36602

Information Notes

☐ _____
☐ _____
☐ _____
☐ _____
☐ _____
☐ _____
☐ _____

Results

Community Foundation

Alabama
38

Monroe County Community Foundation

Website: not available
(251) 743-0000
Email: info@monroecountyfoundation.org
120 Pineville Road, Monroeville, AL 36460

Information Notes

☐ _____
☐ _____
☐ _____
☐ _____
☐ _____
☐ _____
☐ _____

Results

_____
_____
_____
_____
_____

60

Community Foundation

Alabama
39

Morgan County Community Foundation

Website: not available
(256) 355-0000
Email: info@morgancountyfoundation.org
204 2nd Avenue SE, Decatur, AL 35601

Information Notes

Results

Community Foundation

Alabama
40

Randolph County Community Foundation

Website: not available
(256) 357-0000
Email: info@randolphcountyfoundation.org
1 Main Street, Wedowee, AL 36278

Information Notes

- [ ] _____
- [ ] _____
- [ ] _____
- [ ] _____
- [ ] _____
- [ ] _____
- [ ] _____

Results

_____
_____
_____
_____
_____

Community Foundation

Alabama
41

Pike County Community Foundation

Website: not available
(334) 566-0000
Email: info@pikecountyfoundation.org
101 West Church Street, Troy, AL 36081

Information Notes

- [ ] _____
- [ ] _____
- [ ] _____
- [ ] _____
- [ ] _____
- [ ] _____
- [ ] _____

Results

Community Foundation

Alabama
42

St. Clair County Community Foundation

Website: not available
(205) 338-0000
Email: info@stclaircountyfoundation.org
123 5th Avenue, Pell City, AL 35125

Information Notes

☐ _____
☐ _____
☐ _____
☐ _____
☐ _____
☐ _____
☐ _____

Results

Community Foundation

<u>Alabama</u>
43

<u>Shelby County Community Foundation</u>

Website: not available
(205) 669-0000
Email: info@shelbycountyfoundation.org
1234 County Road 11, Pelham, AL 35124

Information Notes

- [ ] _____
- [ ] _____
- [ ] _____
- [ ] _____
- [ ] _____
- [ ] _____
- [ ] _____

Results

Community Foundation

Alabama
44

Sumter County Community Foundation

Website: not available
(205) 652-0000
Email: info@sumtercountyfoundation.org
123 Main Street, Livingston, AL 35470

Information Notes

☐ _____
☐ _____
☐ _____
☐ _____
☐ _____
☐ _____
☐ _____

Results

Community Foundation

Alabama
45

Talladega County Community Foundation

Website: not available
(256) 362-0000
Email: info@talladegacountyfoundation.org
123 Broadway Avenue, Talladega, AL 35160

Information Notes

- [ ] _____
- [ ] _____
- [ ] _____
- [ ] _____
- [ ] _____
- [ ] _____
- [ ] _____

Results

Community Foundation

Alabama
46

Tallapoosa County Community Foundation

Website: not available
(256) 835-0000
Email: info@tallapoosacountyfoundation.org
123 Alabama Street, Dadeville, AL 36853

Information Notes

- [ ] _____
- [ ] _____
- [ ] _____
- [ ] _____
- [ ] _____
- [ ] _____
- [ ] _____

Results

Community Foundation

Alabama
47

Tuscaloosa County Community Foundation

Website: not available
(205) 758-0000
Email: info@tuscaloosacountyfoundation.org
123 University Blvd, Tuscaloosa, AL 35401

Information Notes

☐ _____
☐ _____
☐ _____
☐ _____
☐ _____
☐ _____
☐ _____

Results

_____
_____
_____
_____
_____

Community Foundation

Alabama
48

Washington County Community Foundation

Website: not available
(251) 847-0000
Email: info@washingtoncountyfoundation.org
1 Court Street, Chatom, AL 36518

Information Notes

- [ ] _____
- [ ] _____
- [ ] _____
- [ ] _____
- [ ] _____
- [ ] _____
- [ ] _____

Results

Community Foundation

Alabama
49

Wilcox County Community Foundation

Website: not available
(334) 682-0000
Email: info@wilcoxcountyfoundation.org
123 Camden Avenue, Camden, AL 36726

Information Notes

Results

Community Foundation

Alabama
50

The Greater Brewton Foundation

Website: not available
(251) 867-0000
Email: info@greaterbrewtonfoundation.org
P.O. Box 87, Brewton, AL 36427

Information Notes

☐ _____
☐ _____
☐ _____
☐ _____
☐ _____
☐ _____
☐ _____

Results

Community Foundation

Alabama
51

Friends of McCalla

    Website: not available
    (205) 428-9064
    Email:
    1630 4th Ave North Bessemer, AL 35020

Information Notes

☐ _____
☐ _____
☐ _____
☐ _____
☐ _____
☐ _____
☐ _____

Results

_____
_____
_____
_____
_____

Community Foundation

Alabama
52

West Anniston Foundation

Website: westannistonfdn.org
Phone: (256) 238-9900
Email: westannistonfdn.org
800 Clydesdale Ave, Anniston, AL 36201

Information Notes

- [ ] _____
- [ ] _____
- [ ] _____
- [ ] _____
- [ ] _____
- [ ] _____
- [ ] _____

Results

Scholarships to Look For

Alabama
53

Michael Moody Fitness Scholarship

The Michael Moody Fitness Scholarship offers $1,500 to a high school senior, undergraduate, or graduate student who has demonstrated outstanding achievement, participation, and leadership in school activities and work experience, and interest in pursuing a career in the health and fitness-related fields.

Notes

Results

Scholarships to Look For

Alabama
54

Alabama Environmental Health Association

The Alabama Environmental Health Association (AEHA), Inc. awards a scholarship each year to a junior or senior undergraduate student. To be eligible, applicants must be Alabama residents and either: be pursuing a degree in environmental health; be pursuing a degree with a minimum 20 semester hours of course work in biology, chemistry, environmental science, mathematics or physical science; or be pursuing a degree in any field but has a parent who is a current AEHA member.

Notes

- [ ] _____
- [ ] _____
- [ ] _____
- [ ] _____
- [ ] _____
- [ ] _____
- [ ] _____

Results

Scholarships to Look For

Alabama

55

The Alabama Student Grant Program

The Alabama Student Grant Program is available only to students at an eligible independent Alabama college or university. This is not a need based program. Grant amounts vary from year-to-year based on the availability of funds, but cannot exceed $3,000 per academic year. Applications are available from the financial aid office at the institution you plan to attend. Applicants must be residents of Alabama.

Notes

Results

Scholarships to Look For

Alabama

56

Regions Riding Forward Scholarship Contest

For the opportunity to win an $8,000 scholarship, submit a video or written essay about an individual you know personally (who lives in your community) who has inspired you and helped you build the confidence you need to achieve your goals.

Notes

- [ ] _____
- [ ] _____
- [ ] _____
- [ ] _____
- [ ] _____
- [ ] _____
- [ ] _____

Results

_____
_____
_____
_____
_____

Scholarships to Look For

Alabama
57

Singing for Scholarships

The Singing for Scholarships competition will feature one student per school chosen to represent their respective Baldwin County high school (including City School, private school, and home-schooled students). Each high school conducts its own contest. Scholarships are awarded to the top three participants as well as to each of their high schools. Contestants must be enrolled in any Baldwin County High School program through the competition date to be eligible to compete.

Notes

- [ ] _____
- [ ] _____
- [ ] _____
- [ ] _____
- [ ] _____
- [ ] _____
- [ ] _____

Results

_____
_____
_____
_____
_____

Scholarships to Look For

Alabama

58

Hagan Scholarship Foundation

- Must graduate from a public high school located in a rural area, as defined by counties with fewer than 50,000 residents.
- Must be U.S. citizens and residents of an eligible state.
- Should have attended an eligible public high school for their junior and senior years and be graduating in the upcoming spring.

Notes

☐ _____
☐ _____
☐ _____
☐ _____
☐ _____
☐ _____
☐ _____

Results

_____
_____
_____
_____
_____

80

Scholarships to Look For

Alabama

59

ARRL Charles Clarke Cordle Memorial Scholarship

Applicants of the Charles Clarke Cordle Memorial Scholarship can belong to any active Amateur Radio License Class. Applicants must be a resident of Georgia or Alabama, and plan on attending an institution in Georgia or Alabama. Preference will be given students majoring in electronics, communications ore related fields. In addition, a GPA of at least a 2.5 is required. Applicants must be holding an amateur radio license for at least one year.

Notes

Results

Scholarships to Look For

Alabama

60

The Dream.US Opportunity Scholarship

We believe in breaking down barriers to education, especially for those who face challenges due to their immigration status. Our Opportunity Scholarship is designed for undocumented students living in locked-out states, where accessing higher education seems like an insurmountable obstacle. If you find yourself in such a situation, we are here to open doors for you.

Notes

- [ ] _____
- [ ] _____
- [ ] _____
- [ ] _____
- [ ] _____
- [ ] _____
- [ ] _____

Results

Scholarships to Look For

Alabama

61

JSU Alabama Dr. Perry & Kay Savage Scholarship

The Jacksonville State University Foundation awards the Kay Webb & Perry L., M.D. Family Scholarship annually to students who are children of employees of Alabama Orthopedic & Spine Center. Students from Piedmont, Alabama will have a second preference in the award of this scholarship.

Notes

Results

Scholarships to Look For

Alabama
62

JSU Alabama Farmers & Merchants Bank of Piedmont Scholarship

The Jacksonville State University Foundation awards the Farmers & Merchants Bank Scholarship annually to students from Piedmont, Alabama. Established by the Farmers & Merchants Bank of Piedmont for the benefit of a deserving student from Piedmont.

Notes

- [ ] _____
- [ ] _____
- [ ] _____
- [ ] _____
- [ ] _____
- [ ] _____
- [ ] _____

Results

_____
_____
_____
_____
_____

Scholarships to Look For

Alabama

63

<u>NAJA Scholarships</u>

The National Association of Junior Auxiliaries is made up of nearly 100 Junior Auxiliary Chapters throughout Arkansas, Alabama, Florida, Louisiana, Mississippi, Missouri and Tennessee. The Junior Auxiliary was founded on the principles of helping children and making a difference in their lives; it provides women the opportunity to serve and be a vital part of their communities.

Notes

- [ ] _____
- [ ] _____
- [ ] _____
- [ ] _____
- [ ] _____
- [ ] _____
- [ ] _____

Results

Scholarships to Look For

Alabama

64

RMHC Scholars Scholarship Program

The Ronald McDonald House Charities (RMHC) Scholars Scholarship Program, administered by the Community Foundation of Greater Chattanooga, offers promising students in our 19-county/four-state RMHC service area the opportunity to pursue higher education. This one-year scholarship is available for use at any regionally accredited, non-proprietary, technical, community, or four-year college/university.

Notes

- [ ] _____
- [ ] _____
- [ ] _____
- [ ] _____
- [ ] _____
- [ ] _____
- [ ] _____

Results

_____
_____
_____
_____

Scholarships to Look For

Alabama

65

Jimmy Rane Foundation Scholarship

The Jimmy Rane Foundation Scholarship is dedicated to helping deserving students achieve their dream of a college education. Having awarded 620 scholarships to date, these scholarships have supported students across the United States in prestigious institutions like Auburn, Alabama, University of Pennsylvania, Harvard, and many more. The Foundation's goal is to empower students to excel in their educational pursuits and inspire them to support others in the future.

Notes

Results

Scholarships to Look For

Alabama

66

Corvias Foundation Scholarship for Children of Active-Duty Service Members

High school seniors or students pursuing a GED between the ages of 16-19 with a 3.0 GPA or higher and are the child of active-duty service members are eligible to apply for the Corvias Foundation Scholarship. Applicants must plan to attend an accredited four-year college or university in person, although mostly in person with some online classes is acceptable.

Notes

- ☐ _____
- ☐ _____
- ☐ _____
- ☐ _____
- ☐ _____
- ☐ _____
- ☐ _____

Results

_____
_____
_____
_____

Scholarships to Look For

Alabama
67

CollegeCounts Scholarship Program

The CollegeCounts Scholarship is here to make your college journey more affordable. If you're an Alabama high school student with financial need and plans to attend an Alabama college, this scholarship can provide the funding assistance you need.

Notes

Results

Scholarships to Look For

Alabama

68

Tall Clubs International Student Scholarships

Tall Clubs International Foundation awards annual scholarships to deserving High School Seniors in North America (United States and Canada only). TCI Foundation receives scholarship nominations from Tall Club International's local member clubs and members-at-large across North America. From this pool of nominations, the recipients are selected to receive a $1000 scholarship award from Tall Clubs International Foundation, Inc.

Notes

Results

Scholarships to Look For

Alabama

69

The DYB Scholarship Program

The qualifications for the DYB Scholarship are simple; actually, there is only one qualification - you must have at one time played in a Dixie Youth Baseball franchised league, prior to reaching age 13. There is no relationship between the award of a scholarship and athletic ability. The committee gives weight to such factors as financial need, scholastic record, and citizenship.

Notes

Results

Scholarships to Look For

Alabama
70

Alabama Golf Association Women's Scholarship Fund

Alabama Golf Association Women's Scholarship Fund recipients must attend an accredited college or university and must be enrolled as full-time students carrying a class load of no less than 12 hours per academic semester or quarter unless written permission is obtained from the AGAWSF prior to the commencement of the semester or quarter.

Notes

- [ ] _____
- [ ] _____
- [ ] _____
- [ ] _____
- [ ] _____
- [ ] _____
- [ ] _____

Results

_____
_____
_____
_____

Scholarships to Look For

Alabama
71

Lady Legacy Scholarship

Lady Legacy awards one four-year scholarship each year to a deserving female high school senior, with an interest in golf, who will be attending college in the state of Alabama (The scholarship winner does not have to play golf in college).

Notes

☐ _____
☐ _____
☐ _____
☐ _____
☐ _____
☐ _____
☐ _____

Results

_____
_____
_____
_____

Scholarships to Look For

Alabama
72
AHB Foundation Scholarship

To be eligible for the AHB Foundation Scholarship, applicants must: be a resident of Alabama; be enrolling in, or attending, an accredited community college, technical school, university or approved vocational school in Alabama; and be enrolled in a residential construction-related trade curriculum (with majors including: carpentry; electrical engineering; HVAC; plumbing; masonry; and construction management/technology).

Notes

☐ _____
☐ _____
☐ _____
☐ _____
☐ _____
☐ _____
☐ _____

Results

_____
_____
_____
_____
_____

Scholarships to Look For

Alabama

73

Pen Air Credit Union Scholarship

To be considered for a Pen Air Scholarship, you must: be a primary member of Pen Air Credit Union (the student must be the primary owner of the Pen Air account, not just a joint owner, and the account must be in good standing.); and be a graduating high school senior and will attend an accredited college, university, community college, or technical school, and be considered a full-time student for each semester for the term of this four-year scholarship starting in the upcoming academic year.

Notes

Results

Scholarships to Look For

Alabama
74

NFB Scholarships

The National Federation of the Blind currently offers over 30 $8,000 merit-based scholarships. All scholarships are awarded on the basis of academic excellence, community service, and leadership. Applicants must: be legally blind in both eyes; be a resident of the fifty states, the District of Columbia, or Puerto Rico; be at least 18 by the beginning of July; be pursuing or planning to pursue a full-time, post-secondary course of study in a degree program at a U.S. institution.

Notes

- [ ] _____
- [ ] _____
- [ ] _____
- [ ] _____
- [ ] _____
- [ ] _____
- [ ] _____

Results

_____
_____
_____
_____

Scholarships to Look For

Alabama
75

EnerGIS Scholarship

The EnerGIS Geospatial Scholarship is an exciting opportunity for students engaged in the geospatial sciences. This scholarship aims to support and inspire the next generation of geospatial experts by providing financial assistance to students who are exploring innovative geospatial solutions and methodologies.

Notes

- [ ] _____
- [ ] _____
- [ ] _____
- [ ] _____
- [ ] _____
- [ ] _____
- [ ] _____

Results

Scholarships to Look For

Alabama
76

NATAS Southeast Foundation Scholarship

The National Academy of Television Arts & Sciences Southeast Chapter is dedicated to helping develop the next generation of television professionals. We're looking for students with an innovative vision and a commitment to excellence that will one day "earn an EMMY Award!" All eligible students must be enrolled in a college or university during the coming school year and plan to pursue a career in broadcast or digital media.

Notes

☐ _____
☐ _____
☐ _____
☐ _____
☐ _____
☐ _____
☐ _____

Results

_____
_____
_____
_____
_____

Scholarships to Look For

Alabama

77

CMAA Undergraduate & Graduate Scholarship

The Construction Managers Association of America - South Atlantic Chapter Foundation awards scholarships to students studying architecture, engineering, or construction in Georgia, South Carolina, Tennessee, and Alabama. Applicants must major in an A/E/C field of study at an institution in the South Atlantic Chapter Region (Alabama, Georgia, South Carolina, Tennessee).

Notes

Results

Scholarships to Look For

Alabama
78

Jamie Bax Memorial Scholarship

The Jamie Bax Memorial Scholarship will be awarded annually. (The number and amount of the scholarships available will be dependent on annual funding.) The scholarships awarded are to be used to assist in covering tuition, fees, books, supplies, etc. when going to a college, university, or trade school while having Cystic Fibrosis.

Notes

☐ _____
☐ _____
☐ _____
☐ _____
☐ _____
☐ _____
☐ _____

Results

_____
_____
_____
_____

100

Scholarships to Look For

Alabama
79

Corvias Foundation Scholarship for Spouses of Active-duty Service Members

The Corvias Foundation inspires college-bound students from military families to reach higher. A fierce devotion to education and our commitment to mentoring military-affiliated students for success drive us at every turn. Our scholarships for spouses of active-duty service members offer much-needed flexibility for scholars who juggle the demands of military life while supporting their household and pursuing their career aspirations.

Notes

☐ _____
☐ _____
☐ _____
☐ _____
☐ _____
☐ _____
☐ _____

Results

_____
_____
_____
_____
_____

Scholarships to Look For

Alabama

80

Stuck At Prom Scholarship Contest

Submit your Duck Tape® promwear from now until 12pm ET (noon) on June 5th for a chance to win up to $15,000! Create and wear your original promwear using Duck® Brand Duct Tape and/or Duck® Brand Crafting Tape. Remember to take a high-resolution pic of the big moment! Open to high school students or those in a home school association (at the high-school level) during the current school year

Notes

- [ ] _____
- [ ] _____
- [ ] _____
- [ ] _____
- [ ] _____
- [ ] _____
- [ ] _____

Results

_____
_____
_____
_____

Scholarships to Look For

Alabama

81

ACHE Military Educational Benefits

The Alabama Commission on Higher Education, a statewide 12-member lay board appointed by the Governor, Lieutenant Governor, and Speaker of the House and confirmed by the Senate, is the state agency responsible for the overall statewide planning and coordination of higher education in Alabama, the administration of various student aid programs, and the performance of designated regulatory functions.

Notes

Results

Scholarships to Look For

Alabama

82

David Womack Memorial Alabama & West Virginia LGBT Scholarship

The David Womack Memorial Alabama LGBT Scholarship is a $1,000 scholarship available to any lesbian or gay undergrad student from the states of Alabama or West Virginia. The scholarship applies to attendance at any institute of higher learning in the United States.

Notes

- ☐ _____
- ☐ _____
- ☐ _____
- ☐ _____
- ☐ _____
- ☐ _____
- ☐ _____

Results

_____
_____
_____
_____

Scholarships to Look For

Alabama

83

Epilepsy Reach Education Scholarship Program

The Epilepsy Reach Education Scholarship is awarded to three students who suffer from epilepsy and/or a seizure disorder to help with related expenses for trade school, college, or graduate programs. You must be a legal resident of the United States; Reside in an under-served community in applicable US states; Be/have been diagnosed with epilepsy by a certified physician or must be an immediate family member in the household living with a person diagnosed with epilepsy (parent, spouse, or child).

Notes

- [ ]
- [ ]
- [ ]
- [ ]
- [ ]
- [ ]
- [ ]

Results

Scholarships to Look For

Alabama
84

SEAFWA's Law Enforcement Chief's Scholarship

Annually, SEAFWA's Law Enforcement Chief's Scholarships are awarded to students who advocate for wildlife conservation. There are three scholarships in the amount of $1,000 each available to deserving students. This award is intended for students with a passion for the outdoors and an interest in the management and protection of fish and wildlife resources.

Notes

Results

Scholarships to Look For

Alabama

85

ACHE Alabama Student Assistance Program

The Alabama Commission on Higher Education, a statewide 12-member lay board appointed by the Governor, Lieutenant Governor, and Speaker of the House and confirmed by the Senate, is the state agency responsible for the overall statewide planning and coordination of higher education in Alabama, the administration of various student aid programs, and the performance of designated regulatory functions.

Notes

Results

Scholarships to Look For

Alabama
86

Alabama Scholarships for Dependents of Blind Parents

The VRS Blind and Deaf Program provides specialized assistance to Alabamians statewide through its four major programs: Blind and Low-Vision Services, Deaf and Hard-of-Hearing Services, OASIS (Older Alabamians System of Information and Services), and the Business Enterprise Program. Services are delivered by a team of specialized professionals who are trained in the unique communication issues, technology and culture of this population.

Notes

☐ _____
☐ _____
☐ _____
☐ _____
☐ _____
☐ _____
☐ _____

Results

_____
_____
_____
_____

Scholarships to Look For

Alabama

87

Lettie Pate Whitehead Scholarship Program

The Lettie Pate Whitehead Foundation's scholarship program awards annual grants for the education of deserving female students with financial need at more than 200 accredited educational institutions in Alabama, Florida, Georgia, Louisiana, Mississippi, North Carolina, South Carolina, Tennessee, and Virginia. Lettie Pate Whitehead Foundation grants to award need-based scholarships to Christian women who live in one of the specified states.

Notes

Results

Scholarships to Look For

Alabama

88

Police and Firefighters Survivors Educational Assistance Program

Covers tuition, fees, books, and supplies for undergraduate study at public institutions in Alabama. Intended for dependents and eligible spouses of Alabama police officers and firefighters killed in the line of duty. No limit on the amount awarded to recipients. Applicant must be a dependent or spouse of an Alabama police officer or firefighter killed in the line of duty.

Notes

- [ ] _____
- [ ] _____
- [ ] _____
- [ ] _____
- [ ] _____
- [ ] _____
- [ ] _____

Results

_____
_____
_____
_____
_____

326 Career Profile Books

Occupation and Career Profiles

140 PAGES.
TWO PARTS

PART 1:
CAREER PROFILE:
ACCOUNTANT, AUDITOR
WHAT THEY DO.
HOW TO BECOME ONE.
MEDIAN PAY.
SKILLS REQUIRED.
SIMILAR OCCUPATIONS.

US BUREAU OF LABOR STATISTICS

PART 2:
LOCAL SCHOLARSHIPS
WHAT ARE LOCAL SCHOLARSHIPS
HOW TO AVOID STUDENT DEBT.
LIST OF ENTITIES TO ASK.
SCHOLARSHIP WORKSHEETS.
450+ LOCAL PHONE NUMBERS.
450+ WEBSITE ADDRESSES.

KENNETH EDLIN
GRADUATED COLLEGE, DEBT-FREE.

HOW TO BECOME AN ACCOUNTANT   DEBT-FREE
- WHAT THEY DO
- HOW TO BECOME ONE
- MEDIAN PAY
- SKILLS REQUIRED
- SIMILAR OCCUPATIONS

CAREER PROFILE
STUDY <u>DEBT-FREE.</u> GET
LOCAL SCHOLARSHIPS
450+ COMMUNITY FOUNDATIONS

326 Career Books with Scholarship Secrets

What Are Career Profile Books

- The US Bureau of Labor Statistics accumulates data on all jobs and careers in the United States of America.

- The data is complex as they take 4,869 common descriptive words, all wage levels, and place them into a "median" pay category, describe what each occupation is expected to do, how to qualify for any career occupation, the skills that are required, and similar occupations which may be an acceptable choice for you.

- The results are 326 specific career profiles.

- We simplified this data into single career profile books.

- If you want to know "How to Become A Registered Nurse" you will find a dedicated book for your career choice.

- Each book describes the simple steps to arrive at your career destination. You find out exactly what they do, how to become one, the median pay, the conditions in which you may work, the skills and expectations required, and a list of similar occupations that may better fit your aspirations.

- Each book lists 40+ people or local places you should consider contacting for local scholarships or grants.

- We include scholarship search Worksheets to help you become organized in your searches.

- We are pleased to offer a sample of listings in each State of the Community Foundations. We offer their direct contact information - website, phone number, and email addresses.

- Remember that you may be going to another State for your career occupational training or college, so you should look at both communities. Your local hometown and the town or region of your College or University.

326 Career and Occupation Books

Accountants and Auditors.
Actors.
Actuaries.
Administrative Services and Facilities Managers.
Adult Basic Secondary Education and ESL Teachers.
Advertising Sales Agents.
Advertising, Promotions, and Marketing Managers.
Aerospace Engineering, Operations Technologists, Technicians.
Aerospace Engineers.
Agricultural and Food Service Technicians.
Agricultural and Food Scientists
Agricultural Engineers.
Agricultural Workers.
Air Traffic Controllers.
Aircraft and Avionics Equipment Mechanics, Technicians.
Airline and Commercial Pilots.
Animal Care and Service Workers.
Announcers and DJs.
Anthropologists and Archeologists.
Arbitrators, Mediators, and Conciliators.
Architects.
Architectural and Engineering Managers.
Archivists, Curators, and Museum Workers.
Art Directors.
Assemblers and Fabricators.
Athletes and Sports Competitors.
Athletic Trainers.
Atmospheric Scientists, Including Meteorologists.
Audiologists.
Automotive Body and Glass Repairers.
Automotive Service Technicians and Mechanics.
Bakers.
Barbers, Hairstylists, and Cosmetologists.
Bartenders.
Bill and Account Collectors.
Biochemists and Biophysicists.
Bioengineers and Biomedical Engineers.
Biological Technicians.
Boilermakers.
Bookkeeping, Accounting, and Auditing Clerks.
Broadcast, Sound, and Video Technicians.
Budget Analysts.
Butchers.
Career and Technical Education Teachers.
Carpenters.
Cartographers and Photogrammetrists.
Cashiers.
Chefs and Head Cooks.
Chemical Engineers.
Chemical Technicians.
Chemists and Materials Scientists.
Childcare Workers.
Chiropractors.
Civil Engineering Technologists, Technicians.
Civil Engineers.

2

Claims Adjusters, Appraisers, Examiners, and Investigators.
Clinical Laboratory Technologists and Technicians.
Coaches and Scouts.
Computer and Information Systems Managers.
Compensation, Benefits, and Job Analysis Specialists.
Computer and Information Research Scientists.
Computer Hardware Engineers.
Computer Network Architects.
Computer Programmers.
Computer Support Specialists.
Computer Systems Analysts.
Conservation Scientists and Foresters.
Construction and Building Inspectors.
Construction Equipment Operators.
Construction Laborers and Helpers.
Construction Managers.
Cooks.
Correctional Officers and Bailiffs
Cost Estimators.
Court Reporters and Simultaneous Captioners.
Craft and Fine Artists.
Customer Service Representatives.
Dancers and Choreographers.
Data Scientists.
Database Administrators and Architects.
Delivery Truck Drivers and Drivers/Sales Workers.
Dental, Ophthalmic Laboratory, Medical Appliance Technicians.
Dental Assistants.
Dental Hygienists.
Dentists.
Desktop Publishers.
Diesel Service Technicians and Mechanics.
Dietitians and Nutritionists.
Drafters.
Drywall Installers, Ceiling Tile Installers, and Tapers.
Economists.
Editors.
Electrical, Electronic Engineering Technologists, Technicians.
Electrical and Electronics Engineers.
Electrical and Electronics Installers and Repairers.
Electricians.
Electro-mechanical, Mechatronics Technologists, Technicians.
Elementary, Middle, and High School Principals.
Elevator and Escalator Installers and Repairers.
Emergency Management Directors.
EMTs and Paramedics.
Environmental Engineering Technologists and Technicians.
Environmental Engineers.
Environmental Science and Protection Technicians.
Environmental Scientists and Specialists.

114

3

Epidemiologists.
Exercise Physiologists.
Farmers, Ranchers, and Other Agricultural Managers.
Fashion Designers.
Film and Video Editors and Camera Operators.
Financial Analysts.
Financial Clerks.
Financial Examiners.
Financial Managers.
Fire Inspectors.
Firefighters.
Fishing and Hunting Workers.
Fitness Trainers and Instructors.
Flight Attendants.
Flooring Installers and Tile and Stone Setters.
Floral Designers.
Food and Beverage Serving and Related Workers.
Food Preparation Workers.
Food Processing Equipment Workers.
Food Service Managers.
Forensic Science Technicians.
Forest and Conservation Workers.
Fundraisers.
Funeral Service Workers.
Gambling Service Workers.
General Maintenance and Repair Workers.
General Office Clerks.
Genetic Counselors.
Geographers.
Geological and Hydrologic Technicians.
Geoscientists.
Glaziers.
Graphic Designers.
Grounds Maintenance Workers.
Hand Laborers and Material Workers.
Hazardous Materials Removal Workers.
Health and Safety Engineers.
Health Education Specialists and Community Health Workers.
Health Information Technologists, Medical Registrars.
Heating, Air Conditioning, Refrigeration Mechanics, Installers.
Heavy and Tractor-trailer Truck Drivers.
Heavy Vehicle and Mobile Equipment Service Technicians.
High School Teachers.
Historians.
Home Health and Personal Care Aides.
Human Resources Managers.
Human Resources Specialists.
Hydrologists.
Industrial Designers.
Industrial Engineering Technologists and Technicians.
Industrial Engineers.
Industrial Machinery Mechanics, Machinery Maintenance Workers, and Millwrights.
Industrial Production Managers.
Information Clerks.
Information Security Analysts.
Instructional Coordinators.
Insulation Workers.

4

Insurance Sales Agents.
Insurance Underwriters.
Interior Designers.
Interpreters and Translators.
Iron Workers.
Janitors and Building Cleaners.
Jewelers and Precious Stone and Metal Workers.
Judges and Hearing Officers.
Kindergarten and Elementary School Teachers.
Labor Relations Specialists.
Landscape Architects.
Lawyers.
Librarians and Library Media Specialists.
Library Technicians and Assistants.
Licensed Practical and Licensed Vocational Nurses.
Line Installers.
Loan Officers.
Lodging Managers.
Logging Workers.
Logisticians.
Machinists and Tool and Die Makers.
Management Analysts.
Manicurists and Pedicurists.
Marine Engineers and Naval Architects.
Market Research Analysts.
Marriage and Family Therapists.
Masonry Workers.
Massage Therapists.
Material Moving Machine Operators.
Material Recording Clerks.
Materials Engineers.

Mathematicians and Statisticians.
Mechanical Engineer.
Mechanical Engineering Technologists and Technicians.
Medical and Health Services Managers.
Medical Assistants.
Medical Equipment Repairers.
Medical Records Specialists.
Medical Scientists.
Medical Sonographers, and Cardiovascular Technologists, Technicians.
Medical Transcriptionists.
Meeting, Convention, and Event Planners.
Metal and Plastic Machine Workers.
Microbiologists.
Middle School Teachers.
Military.
Mining and Geological Engineers
Models.
Music Directors and Composers.
Musicians and Singers.
Natural Sciences Managers.
Network and Computer Systems Administrators.
News Analysts, Reporters, Journalists.
Nuclear Engineers.
Nuclear Medicine Technologists.
Nurse Anesthetists, Nurse Midwives, Nurse Practitioners.
Nursing Assistant and Orderlies.
Occupational Health and Safety Specialists. and Technicians.
Occupational Therapists.

116

5

Occupational Therapy Assistants and Aides.
Operations Research Analysts.
Opticians.
Optometrists.
Orthotists and Prosthetists.
Painters, Construction and Maintenance.
Painting and Coating Workers.
Paralegals and Legal Assistants.
Passenger Vehicle Drivers.
Personal Financial Advisors.
Pest Control Workers.
Petroleum Engineers.
Pharmacists.
Pharmacy Technicians.
Phlebotomists.
Photographers.
Physical Therapist Assistants and Aides.
Physical Therapists.
Physical Assistants.
Physicians and Surgeons.
Physicists and Astronomers.
Plumbers, Pipefitters, and Steamfitters.
Podiatrists.
Police and Detectives.
Political Scientists.
Postal Service Workers.
Postsecondary Education Administrators.
Postsecondary Teachers.
Power Plant Operators, Distributors, and Dispatchers.
Preschool and Childcare Center Directors.
Preschool Teachers.
Private Detectives and Investigators.
Probation Officers, Correctional Treatment Specialists.
Producers and Directors.
Project Management Specialists.
Property Appraisers, Assessors.
Property, Real Estate, Community Association Managers.
Psychiatric Technicians, Aides.
Psychologists.
Public Relations and Fundraising Managers.
Public Relations Specialists.
Public Safety Telecommunicators
Purchasing Managers, Buyers, and Purchasing Agents.
Quality Control Inspectors.
Radiation Therapists.
Radiologic and MRI Technologists.
Railroad Workers.
Real Estate Brokers and Sales Agents.
Receptionists.
Recreation Workers.
Recreational Therapists.
Registered Nurses.
Rehabilitation Counselors.
Respiratory Therapists.
Retail Sales Workers.
Roofers.
Sales Engineers.
Sales Managers.
School and Career Counselors and Advisors.
Secretaries and Administrative Assistants.
Securities, Commodities, Financial Services Sales Agents.

6

Security Guards and Gambling Surveillance Officers.
Sheet Metal Workers.
Skincare Specialists.
Small Engine Mechanics.
Social and Community Service Managers.
Social and Human Service Assistants.
Social Workers.
Sociologists.
Software Developers, Quality Assurance Analysts, Testers.
Solar Photovoltaic Installers.
Special Education Teachers.
Special Effects Artists and Animators.
Speech-Language Pathologists.
Stationary Engineers and Boiler Operators.
Substance Abuse, Behavioral Disorder, and Mental Health Counselors.
Surgical Assistants and Technologists.
Survey Researchers.
Surveying and Mapping Technicians.
Surveyors.
Tax Examiners and Collectors, and Revenue Agents.
Teacher Assistants.
Technical Writers.
Telecommunications Equipment Installers and Repairers.
Tellers.
Top Executives.
Training, Development Managers.
Training and Development Specialists.
Travel Agents.
Umpires, Referees, other Sports Officials.
Urban and regional Planners.
Veterinarians.
Veterinary Assistants and Laboratory Animal Caretakers.
Veterinary Technologists and Technicians.
Waiters and Waitresses.
Water, Wastewater Treatment Plant and System Operators.
Water Transportation Workers.
Web Developers and Digital Designers.
Welders, Cutters, Solderers, and Brazers.
Wholesale and Manufacturing Sales Representatives.
Wind Turbine Technicians.
Woodworkers.
Writers and Authors.
Zoologists, Wildlife Biologists.

326 Career Profiles. Each book includes a sample introductory list of Community Foundations. These are found at <u>Amazon</u> under the book title "How to Become A _____" or under KENNETH EDLIN as they are completed.

118

Other Publications by
KENNETH EDLIN
Available on AMAZON

- **365 DAYS of Thought-Provoking, Stimulating, Useful QUOTES.**
  "It's impossible to love someone enough to make them love you back."

- **SUMMER FUN Coloring Book** for Kids and Adults.

- **ABC and Numbers Coloring Book** for Kids and Adults: 100+ Easy Pictures…

- **FRUIT & VEGETABLES Coloring Book**

- **200+ Things Every Teen Should Know the Truth About**

- **SUN FUN Coloring Book. 100+ Easy-to-Color Pictures About the Sun**: Learn & Color…

- **Everyone Has TWO Hearts:** The Movie Theater of the Mind.

- **Was COVID-19 A Dress Rehearsal For the Next Catastrophe?**

- **The 75 Amazing Parables Jesus Taught Are for Everyone** - Begin to Change Your Thought Life…

- **Create A Coloring Page In ONE Minute or LESS! PROMPTS Created for Canva's Magic Media**

And more…

All Scholarships
Score Card

Name											Amount

_____
_____
_____
_____
_____
_____
_____
_____
_____
_____
_____
_____
_____

GOAL $_____   WON! $_____

www.ingramcontent.com/pod-product-compliance
Lightning Source LLC
Chambersburg PA
CBHW071834210526
45479CB00001B/125